Inchmahome Priory
& The Lake of Menteith
Emma Carver

In this isolated and beautiful spot, on the largest of three islands in the Lake of Menteith, the medieval priory of Inchmahome was built. A variety of trees and flowers surround the romantic ruined buildings, and in the spring the island becomes awash with colour. The lake itself attracts fishermen throughout the season, and in severe winters the smooth waters make a perfect curling rink.

The priory was founded around 1238 for a small community of Augustinian canons by one of the great magnates of the time, Walter Comyn, Earl of Menteith. The adjacent island of Inch Talla was a seat of the ancient earldom of Menteith and the history of the two islands is intimately linked. The priory offered spiritual solace and peace to canons, earls, parishioners and royal visitors alike until the Reformation of 1560 brought the monastic life to a close.

The priory buildings from the north west

A Guided Tour

*Six ages shall their course have run
Ere thirty years expire,
Since first I [the priory] hail'd the rising sun,
Admired his setting fire.*

from Rev. W.M. Stirling's poem *Inschemachame* (1815)

Although the priory church and its associated buildings are now only seen in a fragmentary state, enough remains to make it possible to understand how the canons lived here.

The buildings follow the standard plan of a **church** flanked by domestic buildings arranged around a **cloister** - encouraging the feeling of living an enclosed life. This plan was derived from the Benedictine monasteries on the Continent and forms the basic layout of most monastic foundations.

The siting of the priory and the architecture too reflect the popular religious ideals of the day - those of isolation and simplicity.

These three important concepts - the monastic layout, the simple architecture and the isolated setting - can be seen wonderfully expressed here at Inchmahome, otherwise known as 'the isle of rest'.

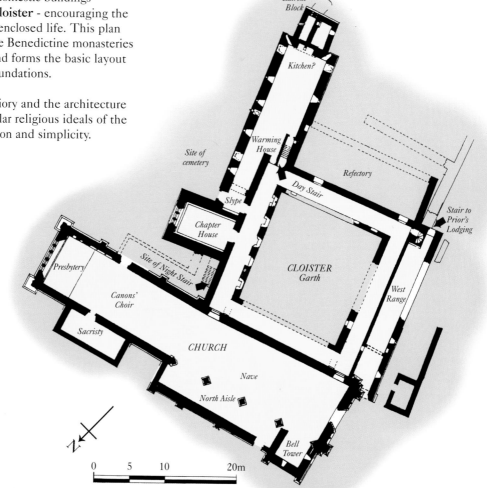

Latrine Block

Kitchen?

Site of cemetery

Warming House

Refectory

Day Stair

Slype

Stair to Prior's Lodging

Chapter House

CLOISTER Garth

Presbytery

Site of Night Stair

West Range

Canons' Choir

Sacristy

CHURCH

Nave

North Aisle

Bell Tower

0   5   10   20m

A Place
of Worship

THE PRIORY CHURCH

The priory **church** was at the very heart of all the activity on the island. It was where the canons spent most of their day. It was also the only public space within the monastic precinct. This fact did not go unobserved by the builders, as the **west front** with its fine processional doorway admirably shows. Interestingly, judging by the style of the door and other architectural features within the church, it may well be that the masons employed here had come from the newly-completed cathedral church at Dunblane. The pier mouldings in the nave too draw for inspiration on those of the richer Augustinian foundation at Holyrood in Edinburgh. As with other architectural features in the church, such as the aisle piers and their arches, these were probably modelled and dressed at the quarry where the stone came from before being brought to the island.

THE NAVE

The western half of the church, the **nave**, served as the place of worship for the laity - the earl and countess of Menteith, their family and retainers living on the neighbouring island of Inch Talla, and perhaps other parishioners living by the shore of the loch, just a short boat trip away. Most would have entered the church through a modest door in the north wall (the far grander west door was used only on special occasions) and worshipped standing in the nave. On occasion, though, the earl and countess and their immediate family may have been permitted to sit with the canons in their choir.

The nave has some curious features. It is slightly lop-sided for the south wall has been rebuilt at some stage and not set parallel with the north arcade. All that remains of the south wall's original alignment is a stub of wall protruding from the west wall. The **bell tower** is another oddity (see the photograph on page 25), as it has been slotted into the last bay of the aisle on the north side at a later date.

Left: The west front and fine processional doorway of the priory church.

Above: The mouldings on the piers in the north aisle may have been inspired by the Augustinian abbey at Holyrood.

Left: The west front and processional doorway of Dunblane Cathedral. The link with Inchmahome is obvious.

This reconstruction drawing shows h
the church may have looked when in
use. The scene is a requiem mass for
of the Menteith family. The walls are
plastered and painted and the windo
filled with coloured glass. Two carve
stone faces watch from the fine five-l
lancet window. The canons are in th
stalls lining the choir, whilst a group
mourners stand on the other side of
richly carved wooden rood screen the
separates choir from nave. The coffi
of the deceased stands before the
altar, on a bier and beneath a pall
(David Simon).

THE CHOIR

The **choir** in the eastern half of the church was the preserve of the canons. It was formally closed off from the nave by a **rood screen** (so-called because it had a giant rood, or crucifix, placed on it). By passing through this screen, you were taking an important step - from the temporal world into the private world of the religious.

Here in their choir the canons passed much of their waking day, in their wooden stalls, or seats, placed along the side-walls, listening, praying, watching, singing and chanting. For much of that time their attention was focused on the **presbytery**, at the east end, where the high altar lay. Imagine the scene as dawn broke and sunlight poured in through the magnificent east window with its five tall lancets.

Set into the south wall of the presbytery are three architectural features used during the celebration of the mass. The fine row of three seats, or **sedilia**, was where the celebrant (sitting in the highest seat) and his assistants sat at certain points during the service.

Further along the wall is the **piscina**, or basin, in which the priest ritually rinsed his hands and washed the sacred vessels during the mass. The water drained through the stone basin into the ground outside the church, thus ensuring that everything associated with the transformation of bread and wine into the body and blood of Christ during the mass remained on consecrated ground. The **aumbry**, or small cupboard, beyond was perhaps the Easter Sepulchre where the reserved sacrament and crucifix from Good Friday were kept safe till Easter Day.

The door through the north wall led to the **sacristy**, a lean-to building of which only the lower courses remain. The priestly vestments and sacred vessels used for the mass were stored here, in securely padlocked and iron-bound chests.

One of the fine stone faces peering down from the lancet window at the east end.

The sedilia (seats) in the choir, and beyond them the piscina and aumbry.

The east end of the priory church with its five-light lancet window.

The interment of R.B.Cunninghame Graham (inset) in the ancient priory in 1936.
(Courtesy of Getty Images; and The Scottish Media Group/SCRAN.)

THE WALL-PLAQUES
AND GRAVESLABS

The **commemorative wall-plaques** and **graveslabs** in the choir today are post-monastic, and belong in the main to members of the Graham family.

Perhaps the most well-known is that to R.B. Cunninghame Graham, the famous writer, traveller and politician, who was interred here in 1936 alongside his wife. Cunninghame Graham co-founded, with Keir Hardie, the Scottish Labour Party in 1888, and the National Party of Scotland in 1928, and went on to become the first President of the Scottish National Party in 1934.

When the Augustinians were in residence, the choir would have been reserved for the burial of the Earl and Countess of Menteith and members of their family. The charming double effigy of Earl Walter and his lady, Mary, on display in the chapter house (see page 13), formerly lay in the centre of the choir, as the engraving on page 27 clearly shows. The priors of Inchmahome would have been interred in the chapter house, whilst the canons themselves were laid to rest in the cemetery to its east.

Leaving by the door in the south wall of the choir, you follow the route the canons took back to their dormitory after the night-time service.

A Monastic Home

THE CLOISTER

In common with most monasteries, the buildings at Inchmahome followed closely the plan first laid out by the Benedictines and refined by the Cistercians.

The cloister forms a quadrangle, with the church to the north (so that its lofty bulk did not block out the sun) and three ranges of accommodation to east, south and west. The centre, or **garth**, was an open space in which there might well have been a **garden** providing flowers for the altars in the church. Around this was a cloister walk which, on the east and west sides, was incorporated into the body of the range rather than built against it as a lean-to structure.

Most of the buildings you see now are not contemporary with the early thirteenth-century church; they were added later, around the time the south wall of the church was rebuilt. Consequently they do not line up with the main church building. Traces of the earlier buildings have been found in the area of the refectory.

The most complete structure today is the chapter house, but only because it was converted into a mausoleum for the earls of Menteith in the seventeenth century.

The south range barely survives, but this is where the **refectory**, or dining hall, was located. The foundations to its south and west are the remnants of earlier buildings, perhaps associated with the building of the first church in the thirteenth century.

Little remains of the **west range**, but this was probably where the **cellarer**, the canon responsible for provisioning the priory, had his stores. The flight of steps leading from the cloister in all likeliness led to the **prior's lodging**. This position was often chosen for the head of the community's residence because it was sufficiently close to the main body of the monastery for him to take part in community life whilst being at the point where the buildings were in closest contact with the outside world. The range may also have provided **guest accommodation**.

The cloister around which can be seen the priory church, the chapter house (to the right of the picture) and the scant remains of the west range in the foreground.

THE CHAPTER HOUSE

The **east range** is the best preserved. Here you can see the chapter house, warming house and latrine block, together with the day-stair leading to the canons' dormitory that ran the length of the upper floor.

The chapter house was where the business of the priory took place. Here the canons met daily under the chairmanship of the prior or sub-prior, initially to hear a chapter from the monastic rule being read (hence the name) before attending to the business of the day. They also confessed their sins and received absolution here. The canons sat on the **stone bench** running around the room.

The chapter house was transformed in the eighteenth century when it became the mausoleum for the earls of Menteith. Traditionally this was thought to have been for Lord Kilpont, son of the seventh Earl of the Graham line, who was murdered in the camp of his kinsman, the Marquis of Montrose, in 1644. The recess above the doorway on the outside was designed to hold an armorial panel.

Today the chapter house shelters **effigies** and **gravestones** brought here from the church for their better protection, together with fragments of carved stone that once adorned the priory buildings.

The undoubted highlight is the charming double effigy of Walter Stewart (died 1295) entwined with his countess, Mary; hunting dogs lie at their feet (no.1). A second effigy (no.2) depicts an armed knight with the Stewart arms emblazoned on his shield, possibly Sir John de Menteith, who died in the early fourteenth century. Another fourteenth-century gravestone (no.3) depicts Sir John Drummond carrying a spear and shield; the Drummonds were generous benefactors of the priory, Sir John's father, Malcolm, endowing the priory with his estate of Cardross, near Dumbarton.

Left: The chapter house with the choir of the priory church beyond.

THE LIVING QUARTERS

Moving on from the chapter house is the **slype**, a passage that gave access from the cloister to the east, the probable location of the canons' cemetery and infirmary (both no longer visible). The passage itself may also have served as the **parlour** (from the French *parler*, 'to talk') where discussion was allowed; elsewhere the brethren were vowed to silence. There is a stone seat on the north side.

The **calefactory,** or warming house, with its large double fireplace occupies much of the rest of the east range's ground floor. This was the only room where the canons were permitted to warm themselves in cold weather. It also has a sink, or slop basin, with a drain in its east wall, suggesting that the room may, despite its unusual position, have served as a **kitchen**. This was normally situated to the west of the refectory, or occasionally to its south in a separate building. It may even be that the kitchen belongs to a later house conversion made when monastic life ceased around 1560.

The **dormitory** ran the length of the east range and was reached by day via the **day-stair**. For their night-time service, the canons used a timber night-stair that led directly to the south door into their choir. At the far end of the dormitory from the church was the **necessarium** or latrine block. The latrines emptied directly into the drain at ground level, now visible from the warming house.

The priory complex would have included an **infirmary**, or hospital, where the canons went periodically to be bled by leeches, and where the sick and elderly canons were cared for. The infirmary was normally situated to the east of the east range, beside the **cemetery**, another missing component at Inchmahome. However, the discovery in the late nineteenth century of some 30 human skulls indicates that the cemetery and infirmary may well lie below the grass to the east of the cloister.

The day-stair in the south-east corner of the cloister, used by the brethren during the day. A separate night-stair gave them direct access from the dormitory to the church choir for their night-time service.

Slype

Chapter House

East Cloister Walk

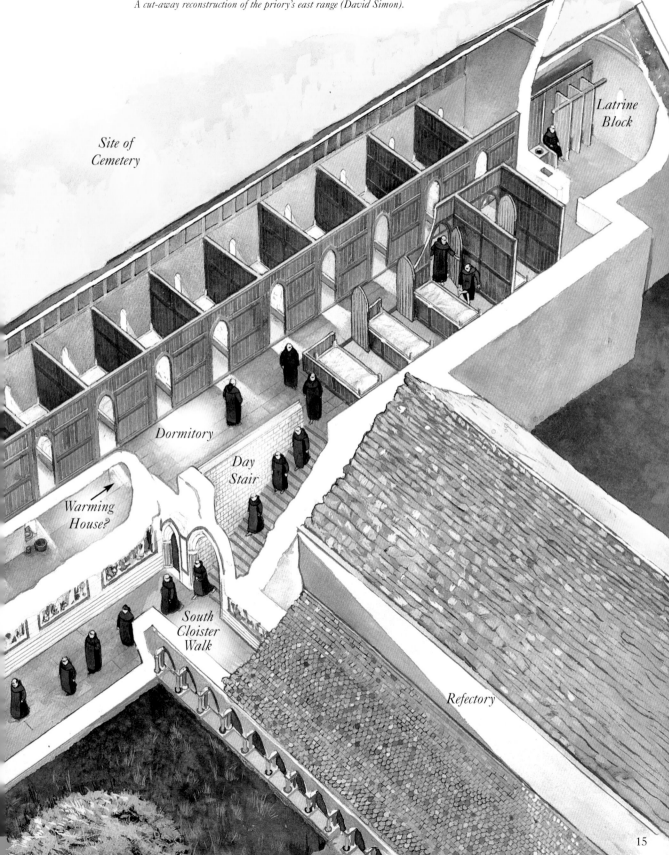

A cut-away reconstruction of the priory's east range (David Simon).

Latrine
Block

Site of
Cemetery

Dormitory

Day
Stair

Warming
House?

South
Cloister
Walk

Refectory

15

THE STORY OF INCHMAHOME
'The Isle of Rest'

'We have ordained that it shall be lawful for the said earl [Walter Comyn, Earl of Menteith]
and his successors to build a house for religious men of the order of St Augustine, in the island of
INCHMAQUHOMOK, without impediment or opposition from the said bishop or his successors.'

There was a church on the island of Inchmahome before the priory was founded in 1238. A passing reference about 1210 to the parson on 'insula Macholem', ('isle of my dear St Colman') appears in the cartulary of Cambuskenneth Abbey, the Augustinian house near Stirling from where the Inchmahome canons came. The existence of this church may have led Walter Comyn, the landowner, to choose this spot for his monastery. But the deciding factor may have been that Inchmahome lay next door to one of his principal residences, Inch Talla.

Inchmahome and the Lake of Menteith from the north-west

THE CANONS ARRIVE

Permission for Walter Comyn, Earl of Menteith, to found a priory on Inchmahome was granted by the bishop of Dunblane and authorised by Pope Gregory IX on 1 July 1238. As with any new foundation, an endowment was necessary to support the prior and canons in their work. This was provided in the first instance by the revenues from two churches: 'and moreover we have assigned, in pure and perpetual alms, to these religious men serving God in the said island, the churches of Leny'. The churches of Kilmadock and Port are also thought to have been donated to the priory, along with at least four chapels. These were probably located on land around the loch, one to the east, one to the west at Arnchly, the third at Chapellaroch to the south west, and the fourth on property belonging to the Drummond family. We cannot be sure that all the chapels were in use at the same time.

Known also as the 'Isle of Rest', the island was ideally suited to the brethren. It offered them isolation and the potential for self-sufficiency, whilst keeping them within reasonable distance of their mother house of Cambuskenneth and the royal castle at Stirling.

The seal of the priory, showing the Virgin Mary cradling the baby Jesus, was attached to a document dated 1562.

Although we understand that the priory flourished from its foundation in 1238 until the Reformation in 1560, no cartulary (collection of records) has survived for Inchmahome itself. Some original charters have survived in other archives - for example, in the cartularies of Cambuskenneth and Arbroath - and we know enough to be able to list a number of the priors. The first on record is Adam, whose name appears on the Ragman Roll, the register of Scots forced to swear allegiance to Edward I of England at Berwick in 1296, at the outset of the Wars of Independence.

An Augustinian canon, as shown in Dugdale's Monasticon.

A LIST OF KNOWN PRIORS	
Adam	1296
Maurice	1297-1309
Cristin	1309 - 1319
Patrick de Port	1419
Patrick de Cardross	1419-1445
Thomas de Arbroath	1419-1420
Maurice de Cardross	1445
Gilbert de Camera (Chalmers)	1450-1468 & 1469
David Noble	1468
Thomas Dog	1469-1477
John Cavers	1470-1473
Alexander Ruch	1474-1479
Walter Drummond	1477
John Ruch	1479

Priors of Inchmahome listed in Watt & Shead's The Heads of Religious Houses in Scotland *(2001). Some of the names overlap, a confusion arising sometimes through contradiction between the records, but also through internal rivalry, an unappealing but growing fact of life in monasteries that led in time to the Reformation.*

Left: The islands of Inchmahome and Inch Talla from the north.

THE AUGUSTINIANS

At the heart of the monastic ideal was the intention that individuals should live a communal life with no private property or possessions, emulating the true apostolic life as described in the *Acts of the Apostles*. This, together with a desire to live away from the temptations that an ordinary life might pose and follow a strict regime, would free the devout to pursue spiritual perfection. These ideals of poverty, chastity and obedience formed the basis of monastic life.

St Augustine (d. 430), bishop of Hippo in north Africa, argued that these should be the aims of the priesthood (that is, not just monks) and adopted the practice in his own church. But after initial espousal, the *Rule of St Augustine* lay dormant for several centuries until the desire to improve clerical discipline, coupled with the feeling that a formal rule would give the priesthood greater coherence, led to its reintroduction. In 1059 the Lateran Council formally recognised the adoption of a common life by the clergy, and groups of clergy who formed such communities came to be known as Augustinian canons or canons *regular* (that is, canons who adopted a rule). They were also known as the Black Canons from the colour of their habit.

Walter Comyn's decision to make Inchmahome an Augustinian foundation was not an isolated one. Largely due to their flexibility, the Augustinians were fast becoming one of the most popular choices among founders of religious houses in Britain. Alexander I introduced the order to Scotland around 1120 with the prestigious foundation at Scone, the ancient king-making centre. His younger brother, David I, continued his work by establishing important houses at St Andrews, Holyrood and elsewhere. In all, eighteen Augustinian houses were established in Scotland between the twelfth and fourteenth centuries.

The canons settling on Inchmahome came from the Augustinian house at Cambuskenneth, near Stirling. Alas, we know little about them as individuals. By this date they need not necessarily have come from aristocratic families, although they would have been of free birth, and in all likelihood have entered the priesthood of their own free will. The Augustinians were noted for their clerical and managerial skills, and for these reasons their priories were often located next to royal castles and other important secular centres.

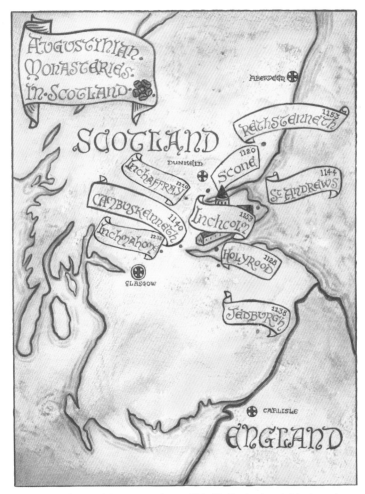

The principal Augustinian monasteries established in Scotland, and their dates of foundation. Some smaller priories have not been included (Michelle McCluskie).

The free standing bell-tower at Cambuskenneth Abbey, with Stirling Castle high on the crag behind. The canons at Inchmahome were brought from Cambuskenneth.

A page from the Murthly Book of Hours. *Books of Hours were devotional tomes made for private use and often beautifully decorated. They were based on the monastic practice of praying at certain hours of the day but were designed for private (mainly aristocratic) use. Research suggests that this particular book may have been made for Joan de Valence, who married John Comyn (III) of Badenoch in 1292 - Walter Comyn, founder of Inchmahome, was his great-great uncle. It may be she who is portrayed in this illumination. (Courtesy of the National Library of Scotland.)*

enteith was one of the great provinces of medieval Scotland, although relatively little is known of its earls prior to 1200. The marriage of Isabella, daughter of the third Earl and Countess of Menteith in her own right, to Walter Comyn, around 1233, led directly to the foundation of Inchmahome Priory, beside Inch Talla, a principal residence of the earldom.

The Comyns enjoyed immense influence in both Scotland and England, but their status was not to last. The 'Comyn century' was brought to an abrupt end in 1306 with the murder of John Comyn (III), in Dumfries, by King Robert Bruce (who visited the priory the same year and on two other occasions). But in the middle of the thirteenth century, the Comyns could do no wrong. Walter's marriage to Isabella was a particular high point, and the founding of Inchmahome was Walter's way of announcing that he had 'arrived'. It was also seen as an investment, not simply in temporal terms but more importantly in the family's long-term spiritual well-being.

Walter Comyn's star continued to rise - a contemporary, Matthew Paris, described him as 'a most powerful earl in Scotland' - until his sudden death in 1258 led to a struggle for the earldom. His wife Isabella was implicated in his demise. With accusations of poisoning in the air, in 1261 the estate was wrestled from her and her new husband, Sir John Russell, an Englishman, by Walter's nephew, John (I). A third claimant eventually succeeded in acquiring the earldom when in 1285 the lands were divided between Walter Stewart (who retained the title), the husband of Isabella's younger sister Mary Countess of Menteith, and William, Walter Comyn's great-nephew.

Walter Stewart too was an important figure in royal and political circles and a member of an increasingly important dynasty. He distinguished himself at the Battle of Largs in 1263, when Hakon IV of Norway invaded the west of Scotland, and he and Mary accompanied Princess Margaret, daughter of Alexander III, to Norway in 1282 for her marriage to Eric II. Walter died in 1295 and was buried beside his wife in the choir of the priory church. Their charming double effigy is now on display in the chapter house.

The Menteith title remained in the Stewart family for several generations. In 1361 Robert Stewart, a younger son of Robert II, became the new Earl through marriage to Margaret Graham, the widowed Countess of Menteith. He was later created Duke of Albany and built the mighty castle at Doune, 15 km east of Inchmahome. On his son's execution in 1425, most of the Menteith lands reverted to the Crown but were subsequently returned to the Grahams in the late seventeenth century. Inchmahome has remained with the Grahams ever since.

Above: The double effigy of Earl Walter and Countess Mary, now on display in the chapter house. The couple were buried in the choir of the priory church (see the photograph on page 27).

Left: Doune Castle, built around 1400 by Robert Stewart, Duke of Albany and Earl of Menteith.

A Canon's Day

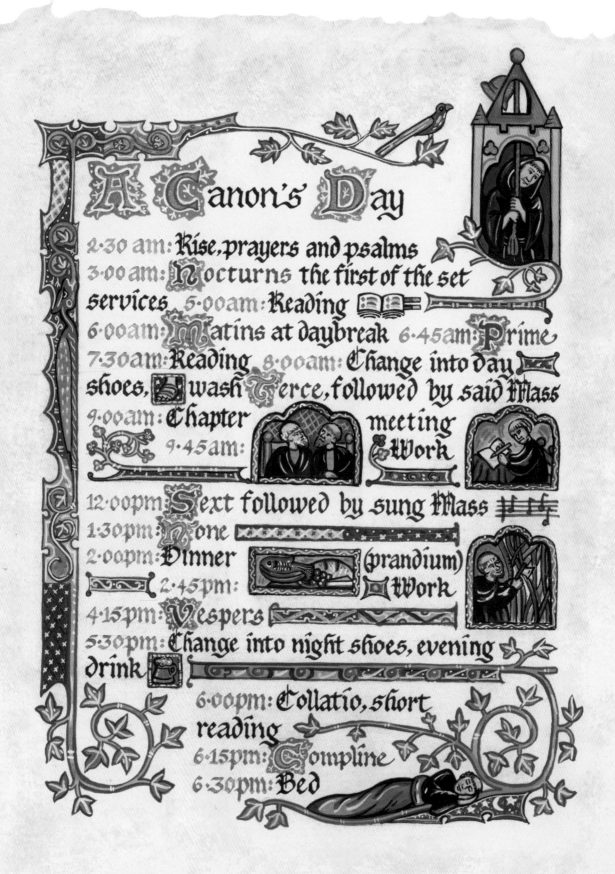

2·30 am: Rise, prayers and psalms

3·00 am: Nocturns the first of the set services   5·00am: Reading

6·00am: Matins at daybreak   6·45am: Prime

7·30am: Reading   8·00am: Change into day shoes, wash Terce, followed by said Mass

9·00am: Chapter meeting   9·45am: Work

12·00pm: Sext followed by sung Mass

1·30pm: None

2·00pm: Dinner (prandium)

2·45pm: Work

4·15pm: Vespers

5·30pm: Change into night shoes, evening drink

6·00pm: Collatio, short reading

6·15pm: Compline

6·30pm: Bed

PRIORY LIFE

There were probably about twelve canons, including the prior, living on Inchmahome at any one time. Their primary function was the *opus dei*, the work of God, achieved through prayer. This varied according to the time of year but essentially consisted of a series of eight services of communal worship spread through the day and night. In the summer the first service was at 1.30 in the morning and in the winter the day began at 2.30. There were also communal and private masses to be celebrated each day.

This framework, devised in the sixth century by St Benedict for his own monks at Monte Cassino in Italy, became known as the *Rule of St Benedict* and continues to underlie the structure of monastic life to this day. Variations and amendments were made through the centuries to accommodate not only changes in ideology but also geography - as the spread of monasticism reached northern climes, for example, the day had to be organised a bit differently.

In addition to attending services, the canons read and studied. Under the *Rule of St Augustine* only a small proportion of the day was given over to manual labour such as tending the orchards and gardens or fishing. The services too were shorter than those of the monks. Certain canons had specific tasks - the cellarer, for example, looked after the provisions, the sacrist maintained the church furnishings and priestly vestments, and the infirmarian supervised the elderly and infirm canons.

Each canon was given a fixed allowance for food, drink and other needs, including 'habit siller' (a clothes' allowance), sometimes a pittance (small bonus), and occasionally their own yard or garden, known as a portion. The number of portions, and therefore the number of monks, was directly dependent on the income of the monastery. Portions were also transferable; the Inchmahome canons, for example, assigned one portion for life to their lay organist.

We know little of the sources and amounts of income appropriated to the priory during its existence. However, in 1561, after the Reformation, its minimum annual income was £1,680, putting it on a par financially with the Cistercian nunnery at North Berwick (£1,880) and the Carthusian monastery at Perth (£1,680). By comparison, the important Augustinian monasteries at Holyrood and Scone commanded annual incomes of over £5,000, whilst the Augustinian canons serving St Andrews Cathedral received more than double that.

A charter from 1604 lists the assets of Inchmahome, Dryburgh and Cambuskenneth as 'lands, baronies, castles, towers, patronages, manor-places, mills, multures, salmon and other fishings, woods, parks, meadows, forests, teinds (tithes), teindsheaves, annual rents etc', giving us some idea of the scope of their holdings in those days. The picture of a small community with relatively large holdings probably explains the attempt made in 1508 to allocate Inchmahome's revenues to the newly built and expensive Chapel Royal in Stirling Castle, a union dissolved within 20 years.

The priory church from the north west. The tall structure in the foreground was the bell tower. The peace and quiet of Inchmahome would have been continually broken by the tolling of the bells.

A day in the life of an Augustinian canon at [In]mahome (Michelle McCluskie).

A Royal Visitor

In 1547 the Scots were defeated by the English, on the outskirts of Edinburgh. The panic that ensued saw the hurried departure from Stirling Castle to Inchmahome of the dowager Queen Marie of Guise with her daughter, the four-year-old Mary Queen of Scots. The island-priory was a natural choice for not only did it offer sanctuary close to Stirling; it was also under the control of the son of Lord Erskine, little Mary's guardian.

Even though the young queen stayed on the island for just three weeks, stories abound relating to her accomplishments whilst here. Her name is still attached to the little box bower in the centre of the island. We do not know where in the priory the royal party stayed, but the prior's residence in the west range seems the most likely since that was normally where guests resided.

The island's romantic association with Mary reached fever pitch in the nineteenth century. William Fraser, describing the considerable size of the boxwood trees in the bower, writes that 'the desire of tourists to become possessed of the relics of Queen Mary has gradually led to the complete disappearance of nearly the whole of these trees'. New boxwood saplings were planted in 1859.

Mary Queen of Scots (1542-87), by an unknown artist. Mary was just four years old when she was brought to Inchmahome.

The Canons Depart

During the later Middle Ages the abuses in the Church that would eventually bring about the Reformation began to occur. One of these was the growing tendency to appoint commendators as heads of monasteries. These were royal appointments, not members of the religious order, and meant that the hitherto high standards in monastic life declined.

Inchmahome was one such case, the priory having been granted to Robert, Master of Erskine, in 1529. In 1604, James VI formally granted it to the Erskine family in perpetuity. By then the last Augustinian canon had been laid to rest.

An engraving from Rev. W.M. Stirling's book on Inchmahome (1815) showing the ruined priory church. Note the double effigy of the Earl and Countess of Menteith in the foreground.

As the canons' presence on Inchmahome diminished, so the island became increasingly the focus of attention of the noble inhabitants on the neighbouring island of Inch Talla. The Graham family, who acquired Inch Talla and Inchmahome in the late seventeenth century from the Erskines, created gardens and planted trees, some of which can still be seen today.

The Grahams also built a large mausoleum around 1750, transforming the chapter house and adding to it a 40m-long avenue terminating in an elaborate gateway. After the priory passed into state care in 1926, the gateway and avenue were removed and the chapter house and cloister restored to something approaching its original form.

From Rev. W.M. Stirling's poem Inschemachame *(1815)*

But now the olden time is fled,
When peers and princes cam;
Those joyous days away have sped
From faded Inschemachame.

INCHMAHOME TODAY

Today Inchmahome contains a wealth of fine trees, avenues, shrubs and flowers, and visitors are welcome to explore the island. Heading west from the pier, you will see the tree-shrouded island of **Inch Talla**, and perhaps make out the odd wall or two of the fallen castle. Moving on, look out for the hazel stools, noticeable by their huge girth and with their spindly wands reaching for the light.

A short detour inland will bring you to **Queen Mary's Garden and Bower**, dominated by a large box tree. Returning to the shore, the next stretch is characterised by alder and willow and a cluster of large oaks. A gentle amble past **Nun's Hill** in the southern part of the island and a turn to your left along an avenue of sweet chestnut - **Nun's Walk** - will bring you back to the priory.

Although often attributed to the priory, most of the trees and plants on the island are likely to be the descendants of the gardens and orchards created by the earls of Menteith in association with their home on Inch Talla. Some trees, though, may have been planted by the canons.

Inchmahome Priory

& THE LAKE OF MENTEITH

HISTORIC SCOTLAND

THE OFFICIAL SOUVENIR GUIDE

CONTENTS

Edited by Chris Tabraham

Designed by Ramsay Gillies

Photography by David Henrie and Mike Brooks

Illustrations by David Simon and Michelle McCluskie

First published by Historic Scotland 2003

Crown Copyright © Historic Scotland 2003

Reprinted 2007

Printed in Scotland from sustainable material by

The House, Edinburgh

ISBN 1 903570 74 3

HISTORIC SCOTLAND

The many ancient **hazel** stools (see bottom right) have clearly been managed on a coppice regime for centuries, and the long hazel stems would have had many uses; the donor of a wood to the monks of Coupar Angus Abbey in 1292 reserved the right to 'take wands for making ploughs, wagons, harrows and hedges'. The stools have probably survived because no deer graze on the island. The three **sweet chestnuts** forming the remnant of the avenue known as Nun's Walk were perhaps planted in the sixteenth century too, making them some of the oldest in Scotland.

The eighteenth and nineteenth centuries saw the arrival of the large broad-leaved specimens such as oak, ash and sycamore, followed by the conifers (including a Giant Sequoia), beech and box. At this time also the island was renowned for the Spanish filberts and other fruits such as gooseberries, plums, pears and apples that grew here. It was not until the later twentieth century that the ornamental species of Swedish whitebeam, purple-leafed plum and rowan were brought to the island.

Inchmahome and the Lake of Menteith as it was in the later Middle Ages (Michelle McCluskie).

FROM LOCH TO LAKE

The Lake of Menteith forms a cup into which water drains from the higher ground around it. In geographical terms it is a kettle hole (four kettle holes to be precise), a shallow freshwater loch, for the most part only 10m deep.

The area around has long been of interest to antiquarians, natural historians, fishermen, holiday-makers and pleasure-seekers. The Menteith Hills to the north are littered with cup-and-ring marked stones indicating the presence of an active early prehistoric community. And in a recent survey no less than four crannogs were discovered in the loch, believed to have been built and used in the Iron Age two thousand years ago. Even the Romans passed this way briefly, as their temporary marching camp on the south-west shore of the loch shows.

The later Middle Ages saw the landscape characterised by its prestigious landowners. The earls of Menteith who founded the priory had a residence on Inch Talla, but as space was at a premium there, service offices were built elsewhere. Dog Isle (Inchcuan) was possibly where the hunting dogs were kept, (though it could take its name from Thomas Dog, prior of Inchmahome in the 1470s) and stables and a mill (the latter built in 1671) were situated near the western shore. This area is also said to be where the 'Piper's house' stood. In the early morning the earl's piper would walk backwards and forwards along the shore playing 'the full chorus of his bagpipes such airs as stirred the soul to martial daring or fostered social feeling'. The earls developed the area around Coille-dun (also known as Cowden, perhaps derived from the Gaelic *coll* or *coul*, 'hazel-tree') into a hunting park. At nearby Portend was the Gallows Hill.

On the edge of the loch south of Cowden there is said to be a fine echo - words called out from there can clearly be heard in the priory. The Port of Menteith became a Burgh of Barony in 1466, enabling the inhabitants to hold an annual fair, St Michael's Fair, every September. Despite this development there were still barely any roads here in 1750 when William Roy mapped the area, and it is likely that the Port retained an essentially rural character.

In the nineteenth century the area became popular with tourists. The huge popularity of Sir Walter Scott's poem *The Lady of the Lake*, published in 1810, raised the profile of the whole area (although the 'Lake' referred to is Loch Katrine and not the Lake of Menteith). This, combined with the coming of the railway in 1858, made the loch a highly desirable holiday destination. So popular was it with Victorians visiting from England that they influenced the change of name from 'the Loch of Inchmahome' to 'the Lake of Menteith'!

The Lake of Menteith continues to be popular, particularly with fishermen and those seeking the tranquillity of the ruined priory. In very cold winters, though, that peace can be shattered, albeit not for long, when the loch plays host to an extraordinary sporting extravaganza - the Royal Caledonian Curling Club's 'Grand Match', when well-nigh 3,000 curlers descend on the Lake from all the airts to compete on the finest ice rink in the world!

Fishermen on the Lake of Menteith.

The 'Bonspiel' or 'Grand Match', between the North and the South of Scotland, in progress on the Lake of Menteith in 1925. (Courtesy of the Scottish Media Group/SCRAN.)
Inset: A curling stone dated 1698 belonging to East Linton Curling Club.

FURTHER READING

J. Burton *Monastic and Religious Orders in Britain, 1000-1300* Cambridge University Press (1994)

M. Dilworth *Scottish Monasteries in the late Middle Ages* Edinburgh University Press (1995)

R. Fawcett *Scottish Abbeys and Priories* Historic Scotland/Batsford (1994)

Sir William Fraser *The Red Book of Menteith* Edinburgh (1880)

Jon C. Henderson 'A Survey of crannogs in the Lake of Menteith, Stirlingshire' *Proceedings of the Society of Antiquaries of Scotland,* vol. 128 (1998)

J. Higgitt *The Murthly Hours: Devotion, Literacy and Luxury in Paris, England and the Gaelic West* London: British Library (2000)

C.H. Lawrence *Medieval Monasticism* Longman (1984)

W.M. Stirling *Notes, Historical and Descriptive on the Priory of Inchmahome* (1815)

A. Young *Robert the Bruce's Rivals: The Comyns, 1212-1314* Tuckwell Press (1997)